THE OSPREY ANGLERS   Editor: Clive Gammon

SHARKS

Kevin Linnane

Colour plates by Keith Linsell

OSPREY PUBLISHING LIMITED

First published in 1974 by
Osprey Publishing Ltd., P.O. Box 25
707 Oxford Road, Reading, Berkshire

Series Design: Norman Ball and Paul Bowden

Filmset and printed Offset Litho in Great Britain
by Cox & Wyman Ltd., London, Fakenham
and Reading

Cased edition ISBN 0 85045 236 8
Paper edition ISBN 0 85045 185 X

1. HISTORY OF SHARK ANGLING AROUND THE BRITISH ISLES

Shark angling in the waters around the British Isles is a relatively new form of sport. Whereas fishing for mackerel, cod and pollack along the south coast of England and the west coast of Ireland was quite common all through the nineteenth century, angling specifically for shark does not appear to have been attempted until the early part of the twentieth.

At that time members of the British Sea Angling Club frequently fished from Ballycotton in County Cork for skate, cod, pollack and any other species that happened to come their way. Their catches consisted mostly of pollack, and the Ballycotton boatmen knew that pollack cut into small pieces and thrown overboard attracted bottom-feeding fish such as the highly-prized skate. This type of fishing was normally carried out at anchor so that the fish pieces, or 'chum' as they became known, drifted to the bottom in the vicinity of the boat and acted as groundbait. Before the pollack pieces were thrown overboard they were dried for a while on the deck to improve their quality as an attracting agent. Blue shark, which have always been plentiful in the area, were frequently encountered when bringing pollack to the surface, but as the anglers did not use wire traces, or at best used only very short ones, it is doubtful if many were boated. Eventually some enterprising British angler must have used 3 or 4 ft of wire and landed a number of sharks. Then, around 1914–15, some members started fishing specifically for the blue shark. By allowing the boat to drift with the wind while the boatman continually threw overboard the little bits of dried pollack or mackerel, they found their luck improved. Using Nottingham reels and split cane rods, they appear to have been quite successful in this and by 1925 Ballycotton was gaining quite a reputation as an area for shark angling.

During the 1930s, as anglers experimented with new techniques, people like the Marquis of Sligo and Dr O'Donnell Brown were trying to catch bigger and better shark. Fishing out of Achill Island on the west coast of Ireland in a small, 18-ft wooden boat anchored over a fishing mark, they were the first to use what we now call 'rubby dubby' to attract shark. Mashing up some mackerel and pollack, they would put them overboard in a bag to attract porbeagle, while they continued to bottom-fish for cod, pollack and bream. When a porbeagle made his presence known, either by showing himself on the surface or by chopping in two a cod or pollack on the end of a line, they would put out their shark tackle. Their attempts proved successful: many of the porbeagle they landed weighed over 300 lb. And then, to crown their achievements, on 28 September 1932, O'Donnell Brown brought in a magnificent 365-pounder.

By the early 1950s, Looe in Cornwall had become a well-established centre where, during the summer season, charter-boats using the 'rubby-dubby' system, took out anglers each day to catch the blue shark. Shortly after this, Kinsale in County Cork became a charter-boat centre and so the two major European shark angling centres were established.

Sharks – Some Information

Of the 300-odd species of sharks in the world, only six are found around the British Isles (excluding of course the tope and various dog-fish which are also members of the order).

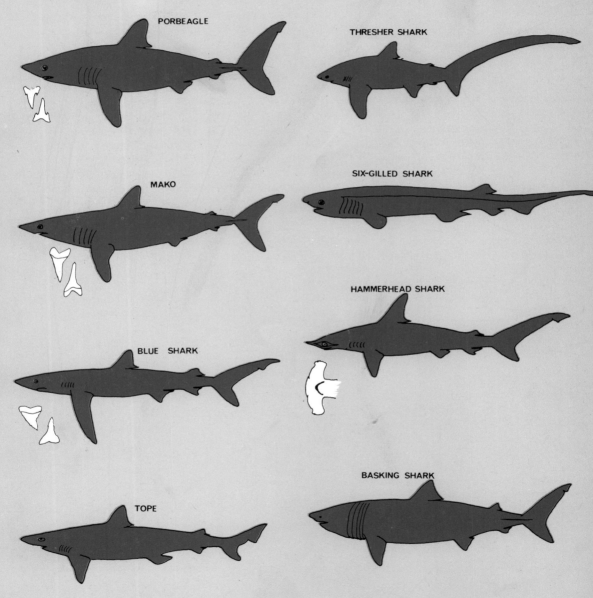

PORBEAGLE

THRESHER SHARK

MAKO

SIX-GILLED SHARK

BLUE SHARK

HAMMERHEAD SHARK

TOPE

BASKING SHARK

4

Sharks are *Selachians*, differing from true fishes in that they have no bones. Their skeleton, like that of skates and rays, is of cartilage. Their gill arrangement also differs from that of the bony fish, in having from five to seven independent gill slits rather than one opening for all the gills. Also, the shark does not have an air bladder which in fish like cod or herring can adjust buoyancy at any depth. This means that if a shark stops swimming he will sink to the bottom, which could be considered a major draw-back.

The shark has a highly developed sense of taste and smell. It is claimed that downstream a shark can scent a substance diluted one part in many millions, and move towards it. Sharks are reputed to have poor eyesight and it is claimed that pilot fish, which frequently swim just in front or alongside many species of shark, actually guide the shark towards his prey when he cannot see it. There is no doubt that some species, such as the blue shark, do not have very good eyesight, but I cannot agree that the porbeagle or the mako are similarly afflicted. However, all sharks have the uncanny ability to home in on wounded or sick fish from very great distances. They seem to have a discrimination that enables them to detect the difference between the vibrations sent out by a healthy fish and those sent out by a struggling or sick fish.

The skin of a shark is quite different from that of a bony fish. Whereas the bony fish is normally covered with scales, the shark's skin is in the form of millions of tiny teeth called denticles, similar in structure to the teeth in his mouth. At one time shark-skin was called shagreen and was used to sand and polish wood as we today would use sandpaper.

The teeth in the shark's mouth are also unique. Instead of being fixed solidly on to the jaw bone, they are continually being replaced from the five or six spare rows which the shark has in reserve in his soft gums. Some time ago, scientists in the USA discovered that in the young of one of the common species the upper teeth were replaced every seven days. Most sharks can, in fact, be identified by their teeth.

2. SHARKS OF WESTERN EUROPE – THEIR IDENTIFICA- TION AND CHARACTERISTICS

The six species of sharks likely to be taken by anglers around the British Isles are the blue shark, porbeagle, mako, thresher, six-gill and hammerhead.

Blue shark (Prionace glauca)

The blue shark is by far the most plentiful of all true sharks in the north-eastern Atlantic. He is easily identifiable by his dark indigo-blue back, bright blue sides and pure white

stomach. His body is long and slender with very large pectoral fins and his snout, which is long and tends to be flattened ventrally, contains numerous small holes. The adult's massive array of teeth are flat and triangular with serrated edges obviously designed for cutting and slicing; the eyes and five gill slits are relatively small. The upper lobe of the tail fin is raked back and at its base, the caudal peduncle, there is a transverse indentation. There are two dorsal fins, the second of which is directly over the anal fin.

The distribution of the blue shark, known also as the great blue and the blue whaler, is almost world-wide. Wherever there are

The jaws of a blue shark displaying a magnificent array of triangular serrated teeth obviously designed for cutting.

A 'Kiss me quick' smile from a blue shark.

'They can't all be monsters', says Peter Green as he weighs this 2 lb. blue before sending it to the lab. for age determination.

temperate seas he is sure to be found. He is largely an oceanic wanderer who visits our coasts every summer, the weather possibly determining his arrival and departure dates. In the summer of 1972 the blue sharks did not arrive until early July, which may be explained by the fact that the sea water temperature in June was approximately 3°C below normal. In his book *Shark Angling in Great Britain*, Brigadier Caunter tells us that blues are to be found about forty miles off shore in early May, not moving inshore until the water warms up during June. On the Irish coast they normally appear off the south-west corner in early June and then spread east past Kinsale and

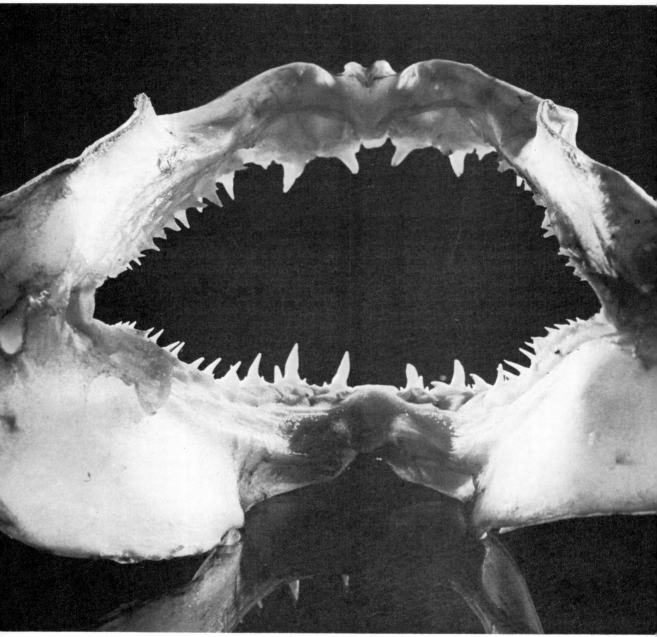

The jaws of a porbeagle showing the long slender teeth with tiny basal cusps designed for gripping and tearing rather than cutting.

Dungarvan, north past Kerry and Achill and, in a fine summer, right up to northern Donegal and across to western Scotland. It is generally considered that the blue shark does not come into water shallower than fifteen fathoms; his preferred residence is the upper layers of the ocean, seldom below a hundred fathoms. However, in 1972 investigations into his

Mako shark (*Isurus oxyrynchus*)
Common hammerhead shark (*Sphyrna zygaena*)

feeding habits gave some interesting results. Work carried out on some sharks taken off Looe revealed that their stomachs contained a number of beaks of a certain type of cuttlefish which normally lives below a hundred fathoms. It was estimated that the cuttlefish had been eaten only five days before the sharks were caught, and as the 100-fathom line is 200 miles away from this point we have some indication of how fast these sharks can travel.

In warmer waters to the south of the British Isles, blue sharks are reputed to grow to more than 20 ft, but here unfortunately, they seldom exceed 200 lb. and the average one taken by anglers weighs only about 40 to 50 lb.

Porbeagle (Lamna nasus)

The porbeagle, sometimes known as the herring shark, the mackerel shark or the bottlenosed shark, is a strong thick-bodied fish with a brownish-grey back and white underside. His tail-fin is vertical with the upper lobe larger than the lower. There is a prominent longitudinal keel on each side of the tail column and just below it, on the tail, a secondary smaller keel. The teeth are long, lanceolate and smooth, the adult shark having tiny secondary cusps at the base. The five gill slits and the eyes are much larger proportionately than those of the blue shark. The first dorsal fin starts in front of the back corner of the pectoral.

Like the blue shark the porbeagle prefers the warm oceanic waters but it can tolerate much colder temperatures. He has been found all around our coasts at every time of the year and is fished commercially by Norwegians off the south and west Irish coasts, who use floating longlines as the Danes did some years ago off the East Anglian coast. Whereas the blue shark rarely comes inside fifteen fathoms, the porbeagle will regularly venture into much shallower water – I have seen porbeagle off the coast of Co. Clare in about two fathoms and Mr Jack Shine of Lahinch, Co. Clare has taken them regularly in three to four fathoms off Lahinch. It is interesting to note that while large blue sharks of up to 200 lb. can be found feeding with 15–20 pounders, the same does not apply to porbeagle. Dick

Downes who runs an excellent shark angling service from the Isle of Wight has found that the 200-lb. porbeagle keep strictly to a very special area. Drifting outside of this he found only smaller ones of about 80–100 lb. Fishing out of Achill over a period of one month Dr O'Donnell Brown and his party took six sharks of over 300 lb., the smallest being 210 lb. On the other hand Galway Bay and the Clare coast have only rarely produced a shark of over 200 lb. The average weight here is 80–100 lb. This may indicate a segregation after a certain stage of maturity has been reached, but unfortunately there has not been enough research yet to give us any real information.

Although porbeagle feed on a variety of pelagic and demersal fish, they prefer mackerel, herring and pollock. In the Lonsdale Library edition of *Sea Angling* Dr Brown describes the porbeagle as 'a fool, a clever blind idiot and yet cute – in fact he is an enigma. He comes into quite shallow water, in fact he is everywhere. I have hooked him 170 feet down and on top where I could pat him on the back. They come into Achill at the end of September and they are there at the beginning of December in thousands'. The porbeagle comes into Achill after the large shoals of spawning herring. Some were seen off Achill during the Christmas of 1972, and I have had reports of fishermen taking small fish after Christmas in the Dunmore East herring fishery.

Mako shark (Isurus oxyrynchus)

Every shark angler's dream is to catch a mako. Because of the tremendous fight he puts up when hooked, he is sought by anglers all over the world. He looks very like the porbeagle and is frequently mistaken for one – as Mrs Hetty Eathorne found, when her 352-lb. porbeagle taken off Looe turned out to be a mako. In fact the mako is not quite as portly as the porbeagle and its back is a vivid deep-water blue colour. It does not have the secondary keel on its tail and the second dorsal fin is in front of the small anal fin. The teeth are long and slender, with no basal cusps, and the upper back corner of the pectoral fin is in front of the first dorsal.

The mako is a truly oceanic shark which roams the upper layers of the sea, seldom going below ten fathoms, and feeding voraciously on shoals of mackerel, bonito or herring. Very little is known of his movements except that he is found in the waters around the British Isles every summer, mostly around the entrance to the English Channel and occasionally off the south and west coasts of Ireland. He is a very fierce fighter, frequently jumping clear of the water in his frantic efforts to throw the hook. His tenacity for life is amazing — a fight with a mako lasts many times longer than one with a porbeagle or blue of similar weight. Zane Grey, probably the most famous of all big-game anglers, described the mako as 'the most aristocratic of all sharks. His leaps are prodigious — inconceivably high.' The mako can grow to the colossal weight of over 1,000 lb., the present I.G.F.A. record being 1,000 lb. and the British record 500 lb. In New Zealand waters it is most often taken by trolling but to date this method has not been used here.

Thresher shark (Alopias vulpinus)

Another large shark recorded around our coasts, but less numerous than the mako, is the thresher. Also known as the fox shark, he is easily identifiable by the enormous upper lobe of the scythe-like tail which makes up approximately half his length. He is normally considered a warm-water shark, usually encountered within a few miles of the shore and frequently inside estuaries. As yet little is known of his habits, although he has frequently been observed using his tail in a most unusual fashion to catch his prey. First he swims round and round a shoal of mackerel or herring, herding the fish into a tight clump. When this is done, he suddenly lashes out ferociously with his enormous tail, stunning and injuring the terrified fish which he then leisurely eats. It is also claimed that he uses his tail to flip his food towards his mouth, although I doubt this. The I.G.F.A. record is 922 lb. and the British record 280 lb., but so far only very few of these sharks have been captured by anglers.

Hammerhead shark (Sphyrna zygaena)

A rare visitor to our waters, the hammerhead shark has not yet been landed by anglers, but probably will be before long. He is easily identifiable by his unusually shaped head which is flattened and laterally extruded with the eyes at the extreme end, thus resembling a hammer when looked at from above or below. Although they are naturally a tropical species I have a reliable account of one being hooked in Galway Bay during the summer of 1968. It was played for about two hours but was lost just on the point of gaffing.

Six-gilled shark (Hexanchus griseus)

The six-gilled shark is brownish in colour and has six gills instead of the usual five on the side of its throat. It has a long straight tail and only one dorsal fin, set far back almost over the anal fin. They were thought to be rare visitors to British waters but lately quite a few have been taken by anglers on the south and west coasts of Ireland. Since they are a bottom-feeding shark they are sometimes encountered by anglers not fishing for shark at all, but for skate or other species caught by means of wire traces.

Basking shark (Cetorhinus maximus)

Strictly a plankton feeder and therefore of no interest to anglers, the basking shark is regularly seen all around our coasts during the summer months. His great size has both thrilled and terrified anglers who frequently see this monster of up to 30 ft lazily swimming by the boat with his sail-like dorsal fin gliding through the water. On fine days especially he swims along the surface with his mouth wide open straining vast quantities of water for the minute plankton — on such occasions the first dorsal and the upper lobe of the tail are usually clearly visible above the surface and frequently the tip of the nose also. He is a harmless leviathan if left to himself but beware of approaching too close in a small boat, as a frightened basking shark has been known to raise his tail high above the water and if that tail happens to strike a boat serious damage could result.

3. THE SHARK FISHERMAN'S ARMOURY

Before describing how to catch these sharks I must first list the equipment you will need. As almost 100 per cent of our shark angling is carried on at sea rather than from the shore, the first essential is a boat.

Boats

There are many different designs used for charter all around our coasts, ranging from conventional deep-draught wooden boats to luxurious fibre-glass fast boats with shallow draught. Practically all these however have one thing in common: they have a large un-cluttered well deck from which four to eight anglers can fish with comfort. They are mostly between 30 and 40 ft long and capable of speeds of between 8 and 25 knots, depending on engines and hull designs. There are suggestions that planing hulls which have a very shallow draught are not suitable for shark fishing as they drift too fast but personally I have never experienced this difficulty. In fact, I consider a fast drift to have many advantages.

Since most anglers hire a boat and skipper to take them fishing they should always, before departure, make sure that safety precautions are adequate. These should include an anchor and anchor chain or rope, a compass, a first-aid box, a life-jacket for everybody on board, an up-to-date set of distress flares and, if possible, a ship-to-shore radio and an inflatable life-raft. If these are on board, the engine in good condition, and the skipper with a good knowledge of the area then the angler is sure that all safety precautions have been taken and he can proceed to sea.

Rod, reel, line

Having a good boat, the next essential item is tackle with which to hook and land the species of shark the angler is seeking. There is one criterion. The tackle should be of a standard strong enough to land the shark. I mention this because many anglers are now using lighter and lighter tackle with which to fish, claiming that it is more sporting and that the shark has a better chance of getting away. This is undoubtedly very enjoyable for the angler but not for the unfortunate shark which succeeds in breaking the line and escaping with the hook, 10 to 20 ft of wire and a length of line, all firmly anchored in his mouth. It must surely cause severe distress to the shark and possibly a slow, lingering death.

The other extreme is the angler who fishes with gear that is too strong and this is very common among shark anglers. I have frequently seen anglers fishing with line of 112-lb. breaking strain in an area in which only blue shark have ever been recorded. I would remind such anglers that were 30-lb. breaking strain line attached to the side of a house it would be physically impossible for them to break that line, using a rod as if they were playing a fish properly. I am not advocating that all shark anglers should use 30-lb. breaking-strain line as all line once knotted or slightly frayed loses a large percentage of its strength, but a useful guide is a maximum of 50-lb. breaking strain for blue shark, 80-lb. for porbeagle and 112-lb. for mako, thresher and hammerhead.

As the rod and reel should match the line as much as possible the line capacity of the reel must also be taken into account. The

A Hardy sidewinder No. 2 and a Penn 4/0 are sufficient for any blue shark as demonstrated by Peter Green.

majority of shark anglers now use multiplying reels rather than a centre pin or the Nottingham type, as they are much easier to play a shark with. There are many excellent makes on the market such as Penn, Ocean city, Tatler, Mitchell and many others. Size and capacity are denoted by number, e.g. 2/0, 4/0, 6/0, etc. For example the Penn 4/0 holds 450 yds of 30-lb. line, the 6/0 400 yds of 50-lb. line and the 9/0 400 yds of 80-lb. line. Most shark rods are made of fibre-glass and there are many excellent brands on the market normally classified as boat-rods, light, medium and heavy. Hardy's light boat-rod has a test curve of 18 lb., the medium 30 lb. and the heavy 45 lb. When angling for sport I normally use: for blue shark, a Penn 4/0 filled with 40–50-lb. breaking-strain line and a Hardy No. 2 (medium) rod; for porbeagle a Penn 6/0 filled with 60–80-lb. line on a Hardy

No. 2; and for anything bigger a Penn 9/0 with 112-lb. line and a Hardy No. 3 (heavy).

Trace

The terminal tackle or trace is of the utmost importance. It must be made of wire as the shark's teeth can quickly cut nylon or Terylene. Traces for blue shark are normally 15 to 20 ft long, of 100- to 200-lb. breaking-strain wire, with 2 or 3 swivels. The reason for the extraordinary length of wire is that the blue frequently rolls up along the trace and if the rough skin comes into contact with the main line it abrades it so badly that it may break. The blue's tail can also break the line if it comes into contact with it. Some anglers now use only 5 or 6 ft of wire and 10–15 ft of very heavy commercial monofilament which makes handling of the shark at close quarters much easier and which is quite resistant to abrasion.

There are many brands of trace wire on the market today, some of which are excellent and some not very good. My own preference is for cable-laid wire without plastic covering. A

13

A dangerous moment — the shark has wrapped itself up along the trace wire. It is at times like this that long traces prove their worth.

good quality cable-laid wire of 150–300-lb. breaking strain is soft, supple, reasonably resistant to kinking and can easily be coiled for storage in a tackle box without fear of its tending to coil when removed. Many of the trace wires are far too stiff and kink too easily, and once badly kinked they are almost impossible to repair. I find that plastic-covered wire gets very tatty after a shark has rolled on it and though the wire itself remains perfect the sight of little bits of plastic hanging off the wire always makes me uneasy.

The wire is normally crimped to the hook or swivel with crimping sleeves and pliers. Some anglers like to knot the wire on to the hook or swivel before crimping, but I feel this is unnecessary as only on very few occasions have I seen a shark lost because of crimp failure. On two occasions I have seen shark lost where anglers, using plastic-covered wire, had not sufficiently tightened the crimps and the wire pulled through the plastic, but this could easily have been avoided if a little more pressure had been applied on the crimping pliers. The swivels should match the wire in strength and, most important of all, they should work when under strain, as a stiff swivel may easily spell disaster in a fight with a good shark.

Hooks should be strong, preferably of

would again remind anglers of the shark that escapes with a hook stuck in its mouth or oesophagus. Available information suggests that its powerful gastric juices can fairly easily dissolve an ordinary metal hook. If, however, the hook is corrosion proof, it will remain embedded for much longer, causing the shark great stress.

Safety in strength

As a powerful lunging shark can drive the rod butt into the angler's groin with amazing force, a rod-butt socket can be very useful. The whole purpose of the socket is to spread the pressure from the rod butt over a large area thus avoiding considerable pain. It also acts as a rod support when the angler is feeling the strain of the contest. A shoulder or kidney harness can be useful when fighting a big shark as it transfers the strain from the arms to the shoulders and back. Fighting chairs are getting more common on our charter-boats every year and I must say they make shark fighting much more comfortable, but I feel they are only necessary for larger shark or for an angler of fairly advanced years.

There are only two other pieces of equipment needed — a pair of gaffs and a heavy implement with which to dispatch the shark quickly and efficiently once he has been landed. Gaffs should be really strong with good sharp points. Too often I have seen gaffs being straightened and handles broken by a lively shark at the side of a boat. Breakaway gaffs, though very expensive, can make handling a large shark very easy because, once gaffed, the head comes free of the handle and leaves the shark tethered to a length of stout rope which if necessary can be tied to a convenient place on the boat. The dispatching instrument, or 'priest' as it is commonly known, can be anything from a hammer to a heavy length of wood. A few sharp blows slightly in advance of the eyes are usually sufficient to turn a twisting, lashing, dangerous shark into a quiet, dead one in a very short time.

Mme Anne Marie Cousin of Paris displays some of the gear essential for playing large shark. The butt socket and shoulder harness takes most of the strain and leaves the hands free to control the line and reel, which in this case is a Mitchel 9/0.

forged steel of approximately size 9/0. They should always be checked before fishing to ensure that there is a good point, as a shark's mouth is very hard in places and a blunt hook is not so easily driven home. There are some hooks on the market today which are reasonably corrosion-proof and on this subject I

4. THE RUBBY-DUBBY SYSTEM: I THE BLUE SHARK

Having described the equipment necessary for shark fishing, I will now list the various methods used in actually going out and catching them. The first of these, and by far the most common, is the rubby-dubby system. The whole idea of rubby dubby is to attract the shark to the bait by getting him to use his very powerful sense of smell or taste. Just as a good hunting dog can smell its prey downwind and move towards it, so too the shark can smell his food downstream and swim towards it. By allowing the boat to drift with the wind and tide this method of fishing can cover a large section of water and increase the chances of a catch.

Preparing the mixture

The essential part of this method is the rubby dubby itself. This is a mixture of fish and oil contained in a bag which is hung over the side of the boat so that, as the boat drifts, it leaves a fishy-smelling slick in the water after it. When the shark meets this trail he smells or tastes the fish and will follow it towards the boat under the false impression that, at the end, there is an easy meal awaiting him. Unfortunately for the shark the first bit of that easy meal he sees is the bait on the angler's line.

The most important ingredient in the rubby-dubby bag is a few well-minced oily fish like mackerel or herring. Pollack and coalfish are not so suitable as they have a very low oil content. The mackerel or herring has to be very well minced and there are two ways of doing this. The first is to use a mincer such as the butcher or housewife uses for mincing meat — though if the charter boat is a regular shark boat the skipper may already have minced the

fish at home in an electric mincer. As most boats run on a 12-volt system it would be difficult to install an electric mincer on board so the old-style hand-mincer will be necessary. The whole mackerel is fed in at the top and comes out with the same consistency as minced meat. The mincer can be mounted on a thwart for this purpose. The other method is to cut the fish into segments of about 1 in. in length, put them in a bucket and thoroughly pound them into a pulp with a stick, which should have a base about 4 in. wide. Both these methods work best if the fish is at least a day old, but a word of warning to anglers who have a tendency to get sea-sick — stay well clear of this operation as the sight and smell from the mixture can be most disturbing. Fish guts have sometimes been used successfully for this purpose as the livers of most fish contain oil.

When about ten mackerel or herring have been well minced the mince is put in a bucket, together with a few fistfuls of bran or other bulky substance and about two cupfuls of fish oil to finish off the mixture. The whole lot is then stirred and put in a bag similar to an onion sack in which there are many small holes and hung over the side so that it dips below the surface as the boat rolls. Onion sacks are ideal for rubby dubby as they are made of material like a fine-mesh net which allows the water to flow in and out of the bag, continuously straining out little bits of the mixture. The oil from the bag will of course remain on the surface of the water forming a visible slick, but the little bits of fish and bran will slowly sink giving the trail a second dimension, and the bran is reputed to release little globules of oil as it slowly sinks. This bag of rubby dubby will be effective for about one hour, depending on the speed of drift and the amount of mixture put in, but it will eventually wear out either by the bag emptying or by the oil washing away. Another bag will then have to be hung overboard immediately for on no account must there be a break in the trail. This could mean that a following shark could lose the scent and change direction away from the boat.

Setting the trail

Since the shark can only follow a scent upstream, attention must be paid to the drift of the boat. Given a particular boat there are four different items which influence the drift: the direction and strength of the wind, and the direction and strength of the tidal current. There are hundreds of combinations which can affect the drift, but as a skipper normally goes to a certain area in which there is a definite current and since he cannot control the wind, the general drift is normally left to chance. There are, however, a few combinations which can be controlled.

But let us first look at the ideal drift, where the wind blows the boat against the tidal current and at an angle of about 45 to 60 degrees from its direction. Since the oil slick, once away from the boat, is affected by tidal current only, this leaves the trail stretching downstream and across the tide. The chances of taking shark are then most favourable as a very wide section of the tidal stream is covered. In some circumstances the boat engine can be used to achieve this. For example, if there is little or no wind blowing, the tide alone is controlling the drift, and the trail simply hangs about the boat and is completely ineffective. Under these conditions, if the boat is driven very slowly against and across the stream the trail can be set properly by slipping the engine into gear at idling speed for about one minute out of every five or ten. The same can be done when there is wind but no current, for example at slack water. By moving the boat across the wind a far superior searching lane can be laid out than if the wind alone were allowed to control the drift. A good trail can sometimes be laid under

these conditions by skilful use of the rudder without need of the engine at all.

I am not suggesting that a good drift is absolutely essential to catch sharks. But I think that careful attention to the drift greatly improves the chances of regularly bringing in good catches. Indeed one of the best days' blue-shark fishing I've ever had was when there was absolutely no wind and the engine was not used to spread the trail. If a boat is fishing in an area where blue shark are plentiful, despite having a very bad drift, a few shark are normally taken.

Preparing the tackle and bait

As the rubby-dubby system is used all round our coasts for blue shark I will now describe what happens when the trail has been laid and the angler is preparing to fish. He has, we presume, a suitably matched rod, reel, line and trace; so his first job is to bait the hook. Around our coasts, many different types of bait are used, mounted on the hooks in different fashions. Herring, pilchard, squid, pollack, cod, pouting, whiting are all used, but mackerel seems to be far the most common, mainly because it is the most readily available. It is always best to use a fresh hook bait, as sharks can be very temperamental at times, mouthing and spitting out the bait for a long time before deciding to take or refuse it. It must be mentioned here that a shark always takes his prey across the body, then turns it and swallows it head first. Therefore it is important in baiting for blue shark that the hook point should be pointing away from the head of the bait fish and towards the tail so that, when the angler strikes, the hook does not have to turn before digging its point into the shark's mouth. Another essential is that the hook point is sticking out of the bait by about half an inch so that it does not get fouled in the bait and fail to penetrate. One simple method of mounting the bait is to pass the hook and wire completely through the fish's body at the tail end and pull the point back again near the gills, so that it is lying clear of the side. The bait can then be straightened out and tied on to the wire to prevent it bunching down on the

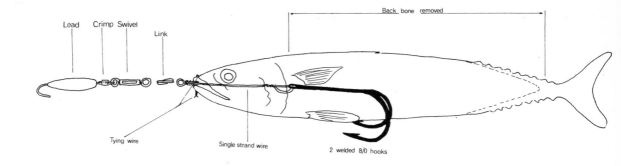

Labels on diagram: Lead | Crimp | Swivel | Link | Back bone removed | Tying wire | Single strand wire | 2 welded 8/0 hooks

*Mackerel mounted for trolling. The hollow
4 oz. lead keeps the bait fishing at approximately
two fathoms.*

hook. Another method is to pass the point through at the back of the head and then simply lash the tail on to the wire with a short length of light line or cotton. Some anglers like to cut open the bait completely and sew the hook and wire inside the fish, leaving only the hook point free. I feel this is unnecessary for blues.

When fishing specifically for blues, however, I find that a half-mackerel is more effective than a whole one. The mackerel is cut in two along the back from head to tail and the tail fins cut off. The hook is then passed through twice and the whole lot lashed to the wire with cotton. I have found that blues seldom mouth this bait but take it directly and swim away, possibly because it is softer than the whole fish and they will take a half fish just as readily.

The line is attached to the end swivel of the trace by either the hangman's knot or the half-blood knot. I use the half-blood because it is easiest but I double the line first before passing it through the swivel, then turn it around itself five or six times before passing it through the first loop beside the swivel. The whole lot is then tightened and the loose end trimmed off.

There is only one thing to do now before the baited trace can be lowered into the water. A float has to be attached to set the bait at the required depth. This can be anything from a Mickey Mouse balloon to a detergent bottle attached to the main line with a link swivel so that it is free to move up and down the line. Once the required amount of line has been let out a float stop must be attached between the float and the rod. A simple match-stick with two half hitches does this job very well, and as the shark is reeled in the match-stick will break when it reaches the rod tip. The bait can be fished at a depth of from two to six fathoms and at a distance of 20–60 yds from the boat, depending on the number of anglers aboard. The ideal number is two, one fishing about 50 yds from the boat at a depth of five fathoms and the other about 30 yds away at three fathoms. But there are often as many as four anglers on board, in which case the floats must be kept as far away from one another as possible to avoid foul-ups. (I have seen some unmerciful tangles because of too many rods fishing, and many sharks have been lost.) The drag on the reel is then set so that just a little pull will allow the line to come off and finally the ratchet is turned on so that, if the angler puts down the rod, the alarm will be raised as soon as the shark takes line. If the rod is to be left unattended for even a short while, however, the angler must make sure that the first run of the shark does not pull it overboard as sometimes happens if it is carelessly placed or the drag set too tightly.

5. THE RUBBY-DUBBY SYSTEM: II THE BLUE SHARK. THE TAKE AND THE FIGHT

The shark arrives

And so at last the trail is laid, the baits are out, and the rods and reels are set and ready. There is nothing to do now but wait for the first shark. This is a very good time to have a cup of tea as it usually takes about an hour for the rubby-dubby trail to attract the first blue. He may announce his arrival in a number of ways. As the oil from the rubby-dubby bag streams away from the boat the water is smoother and less ruffled than on either side so that any disturbance on the surface can be easily seen. The first indication may come when a seagull peacefully sitting on the water picking up little scraps of rubby dubby, suddenly rises with an indignant squawk and peers down at where he has just been sitting. As sharks like to eat seagulls and seagulls do not like sharks, this may mean that a shark has just passed underneath. Or perhaps somebody may see the top of a dark-blue fin cutting through the water. He will automatically shout 'Shark' and point. Then each man's heart misses a beat as he follows the finger in hopeful anticipation that a monster is heading straight for his float. (At this point he should do nothing but check the drag on his reel.) Sometimes the shark will pass up the baits and be suddenly seen just beside the boat heading straight for the rubby-dubby bag, in which case the bag must be got on board at once as he may attack it ferociously and tear it to shreds or even swim away with the whole bag across his mouth. It is very exciting to watch a shark heading for your boat, but while it is happening the angler whose float is nearest the boat should reel in his bait quickly and leave it suspended just over the side. If he is lucky he may even see the shark take it and he will notice that, contrary to myth, the shark does not turn on his side but simply swims over the bait, opens his mouth and takes. There are times when the shark is first seen nosing the floats on top of the water and occasionally I have seen them biting the floats.

The take

However exciting it is to watch these first arrival signs, the best moment by far is when an angler's float suddenly disappears below the surface. This means that the shark has actually taken the bait. The angler must immediately throw off the clutch of the reel to make it free spool, then hold on to the spool with his thumb in anticipation of the first run. The float may bob up and down a few times at first, but this does not mean that the shark has dropped the bait: he simply has not moved away with it. Eventually the float will either go down and stay down, or go steaming along the surface. If it goes along the surface the angler has an immediate indication of the direction of the run and can accordingly prepare for the strike. If the shark runs away from the boat or to one side the angler can feel it through the rod and allow him to take line, but if he swims towards the boat the angler must reel in on light drag until he establishes contact. The same applies when the float is pulled below the surface, although in this case the angler cannot see the direction of the run and must feel it through the rod. If the float disappears and the angler cannot feel anything he must immediately tighten up until he has contact.

At this stage all other baits should be either out of the water or be coming out; otherwise there will be tangles and the shark may take a second or even a third bait, which of course spoils the sport. I have sometimes seen selfish fishermen refuse to take in their baits in case they missed a shark, but fortunately there are very few of this kind.

The strike

Once the blue shark has taken the bait he will usually swim 20 or 30 yds, stop, turn the bait in his mouth and then continue, usually in the same direction. The beginning of the second run is the time to strike. If he does not stop after about 30 yds the angler can assume that the bait has been turned and can strike in any case. In both of these situations the shark is moving away and the hook is ready for driving home. The reel is still running free with the angler controlling the spool with his thumb. He must now tighten the drag firmly (not over-tighten), throw on the engaging clutch, allow the shark to take the strain until the rod is almost parallel with the water, and then strike solidly up and backwards. If in doubt strike a second time to make absolutely sure. This will momentarily stop the shark in its tracks and there is a moment of apprehension.

Have I pulled out or is he on? If it has pulled out that is the end, but if not it is only the beginning. The shark, with the hook firmly embedded, moves away again and the angler settles down to the fight.

The fight

At this stage the angler has no idea what size shark is at the end of his line and, of course, it is the size which determines the course of the fight. A small blue of 50 lb. or under will not normally put up much of a fight and can be brought to gaff in about ten to fifteen minutes, but a bigger one can be very strong. The blue will never jump out of the water when hooked but will fight either by running away or by going deep. As it is the amount of drag that eventually plays out the shark. This should always be watched carefully, it should also be set to give line when pressure equal to about half the breaking strain is applied. This prevents line breakage and allows for reduction in strength from knots or fraying. If the rod has not got a soft button attached to the bottom, a rod socket should be strapped on around the waist to hold the butt. (A kidney or shoulder harness is not normally necessary at this stage unless the shark is obviously well in excess of 100 lb.) It is of the utmost importance not to allow the line to go slack, for if the shark swims across it his rough skin could badly fray or even break it. The rod tip must be kept up all the time and the rod above the reel not allowed to touch the gunwale of the boat as it could easily be smashed.

The shark at this stage is 50 to 100 yds away from the boat, firmly hooked, and moving swiftly — even a thirty pounder will be stripping line from the reel in a long straight run. The larger the shark, the longer this initial run will be, but eventually it will stop as he gets tired. As soon as this happens the angler must start recovering line by repeatedly bringing the rod tip up to the vertical and lowering it quickly, at the same time reeling in as much line as possible. The shark will probably make several runs, each one shorter than the one before, until eventually he will settle into short bursts and lunges trying frantically to detach himself, and will continue doing so until he is brought to the side of the boat. If he rolls up along the trace, twisting and turning violently, the angler will see how a long, strong trace proves its worth. Meanwhile as much line as possible should be recovered until the float appears at the surface, usually close to the boat. When the float stop reaches the tip of the rod a sharp tug on the line just above the reel is sufficient to break the match off and at this point the shark will be visible under the boat. The angler must continue recovering line until the end of the trace is well clear of the water, whereupon the boatman or fellow-angler will catch hold of it. The angler must immediately change the reel to light drag and move to one side and on no account must the rod be left down until the shark has been either gaffed or boated, for if the boatman were to lose his grip of the trace the rod could easily be dragged overboard.

Basking shark (*Cetorhinus maximus*)
Thresher shark (*Alopias vulpinus*)

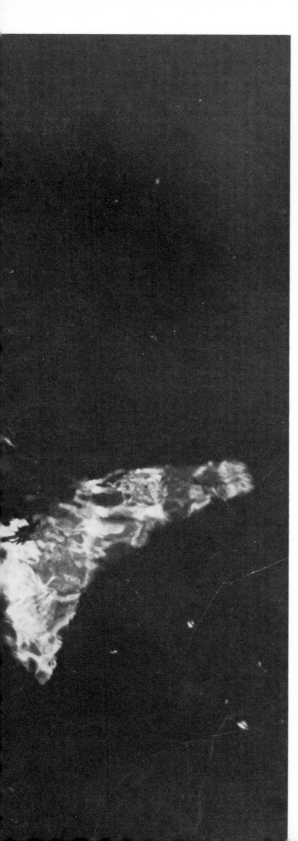

Peter Green admires this 105-lb. blue which he took on a Hardy sidewinder No. 2 and Penn 4/0.

A fine, fighting porbeagle comes up from the depths.

Close handling

Before taking a firm hold of the steel trace the boatman should put on a pair of strong gloves to save his hands. If the shark is obviously tired he can be pulled up by the trace to the surface where he can be held tight until the gaff can be put in. He will be plunging and twisting at the end of the trace, so it is not advisable to wrap the wire around the palm of the hand as a sudden dive could easily do very permanent damage to the fingers. When on the surface, the blue frequently turns on his back and churns the water into foam with his tail as he throws himself about, and if he has not already done so he may regurgitate in his effort to throw the hook, so violently at times that his stomach will protrude from his mouth. When this fury abates it is time to gaff, or, if the shark is small, boat him.

Gaffing

I always try to avoid gaffing fish as I like to return all my fish alive, but if this is not the intention of the angler then a gaff should be used to avoid injury to the anglers and

23

The gaff is driven home just above the vent by Peter Brown, and Peter Green has a firm hold of the tail. They will both then back away from the gunwale, hauling the fish over the side and into the boat. This is the safest way of boating a blue.

Because the first gaff was badly put in, it took two more to land this fish for Gerry McCarthy. One properly placed gaff would have been sufficient.

The author tightens the tailing rope around the body of a porbeagle to make close handling easier.

When it is desired to release a fish alive, it is possible to 'tail' a shark with a rope by first passing it over the rod and down the line, then it is shaken over the dorsal fin and pulled tight around the wrist.

other. He can then pull the tail above the gunwale and with a strong heave back away, and the shark falls into the boat with a thud. If two gaffs are necessary, the first should be driven home below the vent and the second in the vicinity of the pectorals so that the shark can be bodily lifted in by two staunch men, but if the weight is over 100 lb. both gaffs should be driven home in the vicinity of the vent and the shark dragged up tail first over the side and into the boat.

To kill or not to kill

If the angler wishes to return the shark alive to the water then of course a different system is required. The angler must try to avoid any damage other than that already inflicted by the hooking and playing. He must on no account use the gaff for obvious reasons, and he must make every effort to release the shark without lifting him into the boat because of risk of internal damage. Remember that the shark has lived all his life supported by water and if this support is removed and he is allowed to thresh around the bottom of the boat, even for just a short time, the internal organs could easily be damaged and though the shark would appear perfectly healthy when released he could be doomed to die. Lastly the angler must remove the hook and if this is not possible he should cut the trace close to the hook, for if the hook is reasonably corrodible it will not take long for the shark to throw it. The hook position can best be determined when the shark is lying quietly at the side of the boat. If he is lip-hooked, as frequently happens, then the head can be lifted out of the water with the aid of the trace and a small cut along the side of the hook with a sharp knife will allow him to swim free. If the hook is more firmly embedded about the mouth a vice grip can be used to shake it free, but if it is entirely inside the mouth then the wire must be cut. Releasing a shark in a fairly rough sea can be quite dangerous and should only be attempted by an agile person wearing a strong pair of

The author prepares to fix a tag into the dorsal fin of a porbeagle which has been tailed.

boatman. For blues of 50 lb. and under a single gaff is sufficient if it is properly driven home in the area about the vent. The boatman can then raise the shark out of the water by lifting the gaff with one hand and the tail with the

The author and Denis Green remove the hook from a fine porbeagle before returning it alive to the water.

26

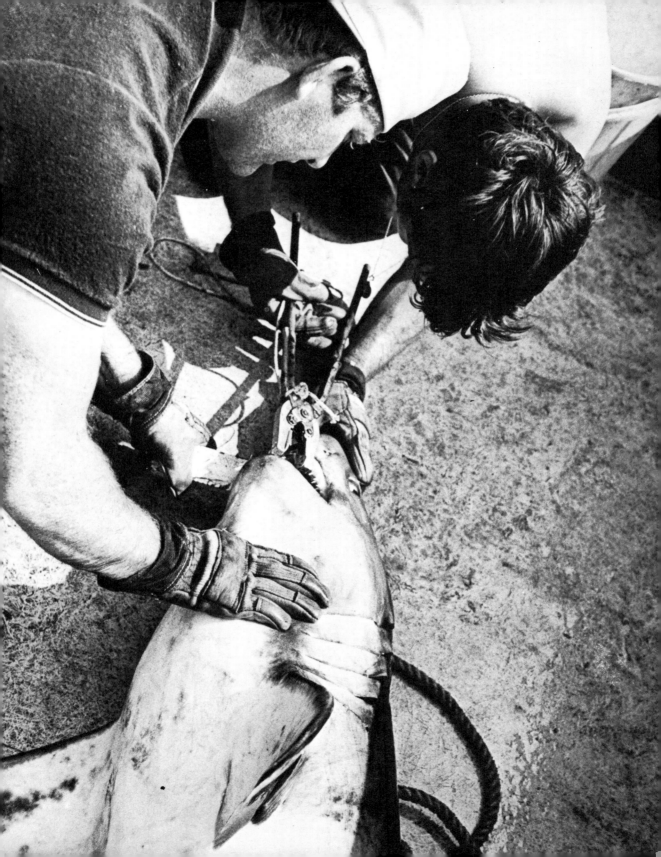

A block of wood between the teeth ensures that the shark cannot bite while the trace is cut as near as possible to the hook.

To kill a shark, a few hard blows between the eyes with any heavy object will normally suffice.

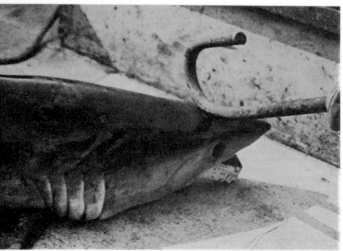

gloves. Many anglers are inclined to kill all their sharks which, of course, they are quite entitled to do, but as shark bodies are seldom put to use I would remind them of the pleasure it gives to watch a shark which has just given good sport being released back to his own environment to fight another day. If the shark is to be killed then this should be done immediately he is taken on board with two or three hard blows on the top of the head between, or just in front of, the eyes.

6. THE RUBBY-DUBBY SYSTEM: III PORBEAGLE AND MAKO

Porbeagle on rubby dubby

Although it is the most common shark in our waters, the blue is not the only one that will follow a rubby-dubby trail. The porbeagle which predominate around the Isle of Wight, Liscannor Bay and Galway Bay, can also be fished in this way. The method of trail setting is exactly the same as for blues but it is a good idea to do a bit of 'chumming' as well. This entails cutting up mackerel, or indeed any fish, into little pieces of about 1 in. across and throwing them overboard one at a time as the boat drifts. The reason for this is that porbeagle appear to be far more voracious feeders than blues and the little segments of fish tend to excite them as they swim up the trail. The trace can be of the same length and design as for blues, except that the wire should be 200-lb. minimum breaking strain, and the baits can be similarly mounted on the hook. As the porbeagle can sometimes be more finicky it is best to cut the bait open and sew the hook into it, leaving only the point protruding. The bait can be fished much deeper, though this will depend on the area. (It is possible, with the help of a 4 or 8 oz. spiral lead to weight the trace, to take porbeagle in ten fathoms — I have frequently done so myself.) Lastly, the float should be just big enough to support the trace and be visible to the angler, for I have on occasions seen pernickety porbeagle apparently put off by large floats.

By far the greatest difference in the behaviour of the blue and porbeagle is the fight that even a small porbeagle of 60 to 80 lb. can put up. Like the blue, he will never jump clear of the water, but after the first few runs he will start boring down vertically with ferocious strength and usually end up directly underneath the boat swimming stubbornly in a circle. While the shark circles beneath the boat, great care must be exercised by the angler to prevent the line being caught up on the rudder, propeller or keel band. The best way to deal with this problem is for the angler to fight the circling porbeagle either from the very stern of the boat or from the bow, so that he can keep the line clear. If the line does get caught, immediate action should be taken by the boatman using a long gaff or boat hook to lift it clear.

Pound for pound, as its build suggests, the porbeagle is a much more powerful fish than the blue, therefore the fight lasts much longer and is far more hectic than with a blue of equal weight. After it has been boated it will continue lashing out with its tail for a long period and even when it is technically dead, anglers should always be wary of the porbeagle's reflex actions.

Mako on rubby dubby

Every year the number of mako shark captured off our coasts is steadily growing, which makes it seem strange that fifteen years ago we did not even realize they were in our waters. Mako have mostly been taken by anglers while fishing for blues at the western end of the English Channel, but of late anglers are beginning to fish specifically for them with quite reasonable results. The truly magnificent fight the mako puts up is something to remember for he is an exceptionally strong swimmer, and his tenacity of life is spectacular as he leaps clear of the water in his frantic efforts to regain his freedom. The trace for mako can be similar to that used for porbeagle but must be stronger. Instead of one crimping sleeve for attaching the swivel or hook, two should be used and the swivels should be of the best and strongest type available. If the angler is fishing specifically for mako his reel should be at least a 9/0 or its equivalent, filled with the best of 120-lb. breaking-strain braided line, because even a 100-lb. mako can travel 300 or 400 yds at a very high speed, screaming off line so fast that the brake linings can be burned. During the final stages of the fight the mako, like the porbeagle, may circle beneath the boat and many fine specimens have been lost because of this when the line gets snagged. I believe there is no more sorrowful sight than that of an angler losing a mako at the side of the boat after a splendid fight of two hours — so once again, both angler and boatman must remain very much on the alert all through the fight. Once a mako is hooked it is a very good idea to start the boat engine so that, as the shark comes near, the boat can be manoeuvred to keep him on one side thus avoiding a break.

Some final points on rubby dubby

For really successful shark fishing with rubby dubby the quality of the trail is of primary importance. Since the whole system is designed to attract the shark to the bait, it stands to reason that the better the attraction, the more sharks will be taken. On no account must the trail be broken, even for three minutes, and the more oil and material in the trail the better. Not only should there be a wide oil slick clearly visible on the surface there should also be a continuous flow of fish particles seen filtering through the rubby-dubby bag. When blue shark are fairly plentiful in an area a good trail can entice up to forty shark per day to a boat where a poor one will produce only about fifteen.

7. TROLLING

The idea

During the late 1950s and early 1960s I was doing a lot of shore spinning for mackerel and pollack on the west coast of Clare with my great friend Jack Shine, a local creamery manager, and his two young sons. We fished mainly from a rocky shore-line called Green Island near Lahinch on the south-western corner of Liscannor Bay, in about five fathoms of water. Our tackle consisted of long beach-casting rods and large fixed-spool reels, capable of casting 4 oz. of lead, and six home-made mackerel feathers 80–100 yds. The lures were made either of white goat's hair or of feathers plucked from one of Jack's white leghorn chickens, tied with blue or red thread. One thing kept irritating us — our tackle was continually being burst apart, and checking on this later we found it to be the work of porbeagle shark. On one occasion while fishing with a long 4-oz. lead, which had accidentally become covered with bright red paint, I saw a porbeagle follow it in-shore, take it with a definite gulp, and swim away, breaking through a 12-lb. line as though it did not exist. The loss of this tackle led Jack Shine to one course of action and me to another. Jack decided to set about catching these porbeagle from the shore in a fashion which I will describe in the next chapter. To me, however, as I was already fishing for porbeagle with rubby dubby near by, this destruction of our tackle indicated that all sharks did not have such a poor eyesight as we had been led to believe.

About one year later, when I was fishing with some friends out of Liscannor, using rubby dubby, we caught a few porbeagle of 80–100 lb. and an 80-lb. blue. On the way back to harbour I laid out the blue beside one of the porbeagle of about the same weight and began comparing the physical characteristics of the two fish. Apart from the differences in length, girth and fins, I noticed the eyes of the porbeagle were much larger than those of the blue. Could it be that the porbeagle uses its eyes more than the blue? In fact, could it be that the porbeagle is a sight-feeder whereas the blue is known to use its sense of smell more than its eyesight? If this were true, why not troll for porbeagle just as we trolled for other sight-feeders such as mackerel or pollack? I decided that nothing beats a trial but a failure and shortly afterwards I arranged with two friends, Jack and Gerard McCarthy, to try out an experiment.

The first trial

We went to sea with five mackerel in a westerly force 5 which was getting stronger, and were at the porbeagle grounds beneath the black cliffs on the southern shore of Liscannor Bay in fifteen minutes. We simply mounted the mackerel as we would for drifting but with the hook at the tail, and started to move under power eastwards with the wind. The bait was about 60 yds behind the boat and one fathom beneath the surface. We were moving at 2 knots most of the time, but when a big wave lifted the boat from behind it increased our speed to 4 or 5 knots and the mackerel could be seen breaking the surface behind the boat.

After about ten minutes, the first shark took with a mighty wallop, Gerard struck immediately and it came away. He was just about to check his bait when the shark took again, but this time he gave the shark about thirty seconds before striking and the hook went home. The shark, a 90-lb. porbeagle, played well and was boated in about twenty minutes. Our second mackerel had just been put out and we were still killing the first shark when the second one took, and so it continued until we had four good porbeagle between 80 and 100 lb. in the boat and only one mackerel left. There was a delay of about fifteen minutes before number five came along and took the bait, but once again Gerard struck too soon and it came away. At that critical point a large wave lifted the stern of the boat and sent us speeding along with the remains of the mackerel still attached to the hook, bouncing along the top of the water. Jack shouted and we turned to see the shark charging along the surface after the bait, throwing himself and jumping at it, but never quite clearing the water. Eventually the bait was dropped back and, of course, he took it with a vengeance and was boated some twenty-five minutes later, bringing our total to five porbeagle for two hours' fishing with five mackerel.

This was sufficient to prove my theory but we repeated the experiment a few times with similar results just to satisfy ourselves.

For the next few years we continued with considerable success trolling for porbeagle in the Clare area, but of course not every day was successful. We found that on some days for no apparent reason the porbeagle simply left the area completely. Nothing would be taken for a week or ten days even though the vast shoals of mackerel and pollack would have remained. Then, suddenly, the porbeagle would return.

There were also days when we simply could not hook the fish at all. They took the mackerel gently, mouthed it for a while and spat it out. This was evident to us through the feel of the line as the boat moved forward. The shark apparently swam along behind the bait, teasing it with little nips, but never actually having a genuine go at it. We tried mounting the mackerel back to front, that is moving tail-first through the water, but with the tail fins clipped. This improved the catch somewhat but not sufficiently, and there were times when we lost a lot of fish. It struck me

that on these occasions the sharks just were not hungry enough, and something more attractive would have to be devised.

A new hook system

In 1970 it became apparent to my employers, The Inland Fisheries Trust, that the time had come for some shark research, so I was sent to County Clare to tag porbeagle, blues, tope and any other shark we came across, in an effort to establish their migratory habits. All through July porbeagle were sparse and we tagged very few, but on 1 August they arrived *en masse*, and I was joined by Leslie Moncrieff and Mike Prichard to help with the task. Leslie was somewhat sceptical of the trolling idea, considering the rubby dubby more effective, but he quickly revised his ideas when on the second day out we contacted ten porbeagle but landed only one. The sharks were obviously there in great numbers and they were interested enough to come and tease the baits but each time Leslie struck, hook and bait just fell out of their mouths. He had been mounting his bait in an American manner. First he sliced the mackerel from the tail to the back of the head on one side of the backbone, then, having removed the entire backbone, he pulled the hook through the mouth, allowing it to hang loose between the two separated sides. He then tied the mouth closed and stuck a piece of light wire through the skull, through a link above the hook, and down through the lower jaw of the mackerel, to prevent it from sliding down on the hook. This rig certainly looked lifelike as it moved through the water at one or two knots with its tail moving as if it were swimming. The hook hanging loose in the body acted as a stabilizer and kept the bait swimming upright.

Apparently, the ten sharks were lost because the hook, getting caught between the sides of the bait, could not be driven home. That evening we went to a local garage and welded the shanks of two hooks together with their bends at about 90 degrees to each other, and the following day we hooked and tagged every shark that came our way.

Bramble shark (*Echinorhinus brucus*)

Six-gilled shark (*Hexanchus griseus*)

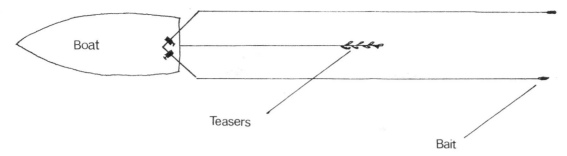

Boat

Teasers

Bait

The trolling system for porbeagle. When a shark appears at the teasers, they are immediately wound in and the shark is then presented with a hook bait which comes from behind.

Most of the fish taken trolling were hooked in this fashion. The hook can easily be removed with a knife and pliers. The porbeagle's rows of teeth are clearly visible.

The author admires a 150-lb. porbeagle which he took trolling off Liscannor, Co. Clare.

Teasers

Leslie and Mike introduced another element into porbeagle trolling. They used teasers. These consisted of a dozen mackerel, without their backbones, attached by the heads to a length of nylon which was towed about thirty yards behind the boat, and they travelled, slapping and banging along the surface, about twenty to thirty yards in front of the hook baits. Whereas rubby dubby is designed to attract by smell, teasers stimulate the porbeagle primarily by sight, and secondly by the vibrations created, which simulate those of an injured fish. The idea was to attract the shark to the surface with the teaser, allow him to snap off one or two fish, pull in the teaser quickly, then suddenly present

Michael Prichard into a good fighting fish off the Clare coast. He is using a 50-lb. class line on a Hardy sidewinder No. 4 and a Penn International with a small kidney harness and butt socket.

him from behind with another mackerel, this time with the hook attached. We first tried this experiment directly beneath the cliffs of Moher where we knew there would be porbeagle and before long a shark appeared behind the teasers. It charged at the end teaser first and snapped it off, then devoured the second. At this point we started hauling the remainder in by hand but found we could not do so fast enough, for just as it reached the back of the boat the shark snapped off and ate the eight mackerel. When it was presented with the hook, the shark was of course simply too full to take any notice of it. By reducing the number of teasers and by hauling

in faster, we eventually overcame this problem and found the system worked quite well. We established that teasers did attract porbeagle to the surface from fairly deep down, and that then they could be taken by a trolled bait.

Advantages of trolling

Compared with the rubby-dubby system, trolling for shark has many great advantages. Since my job was to tag the sharks and return them unharmed to the water, the most important advantage for me was that all the sharks were lip-hooked. This meant that the hooks could be removed easily thus avoiding the sort of damage which could occur if the trace had to be cut and the hook left.

Porbeagle shark taken on the troll fight

Leslie Moncrieff with a porbeagle of over 150 lb. which he took trolling.

Trolling for porbeagle beneath the cliffs of Moher, Co. Clare. The centre rod is used to troll the teasers. This area is particularly good for porbeagle and, as can be seen from this picture, would be impossible to fish using the rubby-dubby system.

with much more pugnacity as Leslie Moncrieff discovered when a hundred and twenty-pounder led him a merry dance from the stern of the boat. During the fight, which lasted over thirty minutes, the line, screaming from his 6/0, badly burned his fingers, but when the shark was eventually landed he said he had just had a better fight than he had experienced shortly before from a 200-lb. tuna which he caught off Madeira.

Another very important advantage which trolling has over rubby dubby is that it allows the angler to fish in certain areas which would be impossible with other systems. For example, one of the most productive places along the

Clare coast is a small area directly beneath the cliffs of Moher which is only about two miles long by one mile wide. As the area runs approximately north-east by south-west a south-westerly or north-easterly wind would be essential to drift across the area, and in any case the drift would be very short. Trolling allows the angler to fish the area thoroughly for as long as he wishes, and also to pick out the best positions within the area and fish them.

(While trolling with Leslie we found that almost every time we passed over a certain small rocky pinnacle we took a fish, so we concentrated on this spot and took many shark from it. We also noticed that when we hooked a porbeagle near it, the shark would immediately turn back towards the rock as if it were his normal place of residence.)

Trolling has another very important advantage in that there are none of those horribly nauseating rubby-dubby smells involved. There is no need to mince up mackerel and mix it with oil, a job which has made many an angler violently ill.

Yet another advantage is that one needs to use only a few mackerel or herring, and even pollack will be taken.

Deep trolling

Porbeagle are thought to be a deeper-water shark than blues or mako. Their grounds off Clare are mostly around fifteen fathoms deep, and trolling a fathom or two beneath the surface there seems to attract them from the bottom. However, if the area is deeper than this it may be necessary to get the trolled bait down deeper, which poses a number of problems. Setting a target of ten to twelve fathoms, I have found paravanes and other such devices completely useless; also, if one were to attach lead to the main line so much would be necessary that fishing would become impossible. A break-away system is therefore required, the principle behind which is a very heavy lead attached by a strong line or rope to a fixed point near the bow of the boat at the required depth. The main line runs from the rod, placed near the stern, down to this heavy lead on to which it is attached with some light nylon. From here the main line runs back to the trace which can be any distance behind the lead. When a shark takes the bait the light nylon breaks easily so that the angler is left with a direct line, without lead, to the shark. For deep trolling I find that a 36-lb. ball of lead allows me to troll a bait at 2 knots at a depth of twelve fathoms or more, which is sufficient for most purposes. When a shark takes, it is necessary to haul up the lead immediately to prevent fouling.

Trolling for other sharks

While trolling, I have never hooked any type of shark other than porbeagle, tope and the odd blue, but I feel the method could also work efficiently with mako. Reading the various press reports over the last few years on the capture of mako I have noticed that many were taken in very rough conditions when the angler was fishing for blue shark. This suggests that the mako, like the porbeagle, is more inclined to take a moving bait than one simply suspended in mid-water. Brigadier Caunter states that off the coasts of New Zealand, where mako are fairly numerous, members of the Mako Club troll with success. I have little doubt that in the area off Looe in Cornwall deep trolling would not disappoint a dedicated angler, but he would need to have great patience as there would be many sharkless days.

I also feel threshers could be taken in a similar fashion, but so little is known about them that it is difficult to be positive.

8. SHORE FISHING

There is no doubt that the greatest sensation in shark angling over the past few years was caused by the consistent successes of Jack Shine in catching porbeagle from the shore, but so far this extraordinary type of fishing has been successful only on the Clare coast. I have no doubt that in the near future it will be repeated elsewhere, possibly on the Mayo or Kerry coast in Ireland or the Isle of Wight or Welsh coast. Jack Shine was not the first European angler to catch a shark from the shore — they have been often landed by accident, as was a blue shark taken off Chesil Beach near Weymouth. However, Jack is the only angler that I know of who has set out specifically to do so and with marked success.

As I mentioned in the last chapter, this all started at Green Island in Liscannor Bay following the loss of numerous sets of mackerel traces to porbeagle. Jack's ambition was to land a 100-lb. shark from the shore, and to many local anglers he appeared quite mad when he announced his intention to do so with an 8-ft fibre-glass spinning rod, a Luxor fixed-spool reel loaded with 400 yds of 19-lb. breaking-strain monofilament and a 7-ft steel trace. His bait was the tail half of a mackerel which he cast out about 60 yds and slowly retrieved. In two months he had proved that he was not mad by landing three porbeagle of 77 lb., 75 lb. and 91 lb. Not bad for a beginner. But for further experiments he had to wait for the following season, the summer of 1963.

In late May he hooked and lost a shark of about 120 lb. which stripped the 400 yds of line almost to the end before turning. The shark was lost just out of gaff's reach after 45 minutes of hectic battle when the 90-lb.

breaking-strain wire parted in the shark's mouth. This experience told him that sharks of 100 lb. and more were not only possible but very probable. He realized his tackle would require some changes for he considered it sheer luck that he had managed to coax this particular shark so far inshore on 19-lb. line. Because there were many jagged rocks visible above water on both sides of the fishing spot and several under-water reefs close in, Jack decided to increase the breaking strain of his line to overcome the possibility of snagging when the porbeagle, towards the end of the battle, started boring down to the bottom. The equipment he chose then and which he still uses is an ordinary 12-ft beach-casting rod of 6-lb. test curve and a 6½-in. Alvey side-cast reel with two spools, one containing 400 yds of 31-lb. breaking-strain monofilament and the other, which he rarely uses, containing 400 yds of 60-lb. line. The 12-ft rod allows him to place his 10-ft wire trace and half mackerel anywhere he wants within a seventy-five-yards radius.

That season, with this equipment, he realized his '100-lb.-plus' ambition, not once but four times, finishing up the season with a magnificent pair of one hundred and thirty- and one hundred and thirty-eight-pounders as well as numerous tiddlers of under 90 lb. The following year his ambition climbed from 100 to 200 lb. but this has not yet been realized — though he has taken sharks of 140 and 145 lb.

In August of 1967 he had an extraordinary battle with a shark, which I witnessed and will never forget. In the previous week he had taken a 145-lb. porbeagle on 31-lb. line without much difficulty, but on this occasion he had only the 60-lb. spool with him, one

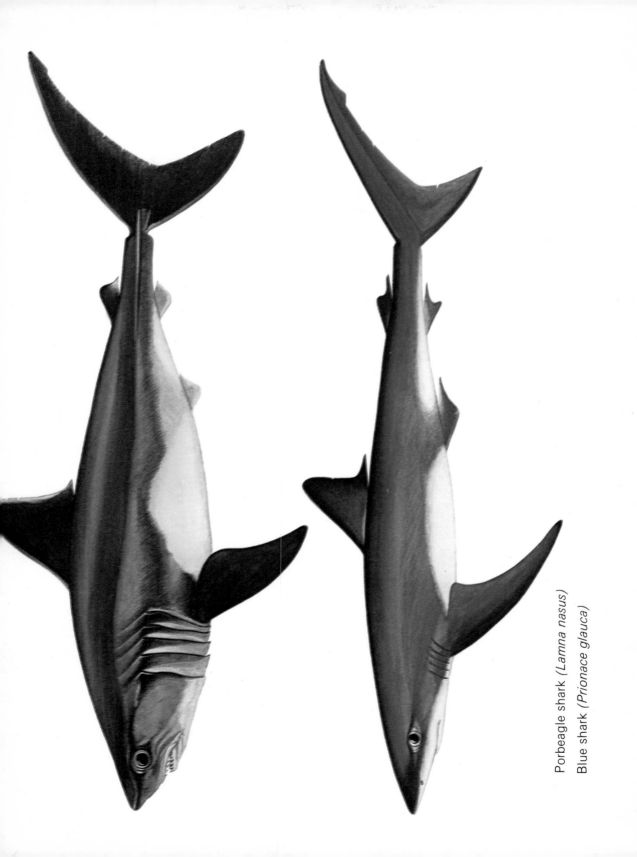

Porbeagle shark (*Lamna nasus*)
Blue shark (*Prionace glauca*)

which he seldom used. He saw the porbeagle take the bait and move off to sea slowly. According to his practice he allowed the shark plenty of time before striking, but when he did, the shark simply continued moving in the same direction. At 200 yds he decided it was time to turn the shark so he started applying pressure, but to no avail: he went on as he was going. At 300 yds the reel drag was on to its maximum and the line was still streaming off, and at about 375 yards he called one of his sons to hold the spool on the reel and try to prevent it turning. But the end

The first gaff is driven home in one of Jack Shine's shore-caught porbeagle.

of the line was in sight, and the shark continued to take it until the spool was empty except for the knotted end; then the line began to stretch and stretch till finally with a horrible twang it snapped at the reel. Jack sat down completely bewildered at the strength and size of this shark. Since the week before he had turned a one hundred and forty-five-pounder in 250 yards on 31-lb. line and landed him, what size of shark, he thought, could take his 400 yards of 60-lb. line to the very end and break it with so little trouble?

43

Jack Shine proudly poses with his best shore-caught shark to date — a 145-lb. porbeagle which he took from Green Island, on the southern corner of Liscannor Bay, Co. Clare.

He considers the fish to have been 300 lb. or more.

Jack has proved that it is possible to take porbeagle not only at Green Island but in several other parts of a 60-mile stretch up the Clare coast. It seems sad therefore that he does not travel more to show that it is also possible in other areas of the British Isles. His experiences are invaluable to any angler with the courage to attempt this form of shark angling. He has learned that it is essential to give the shark plenty of line at first so that he fights far out from the shore where the water is free of obstructions. He plays the fish almost to a standstill so that only a little

pressure on the line manoeuvres him into a gaffing position. He then uses two gaffs of 9–12 ft made up of graded sewer sticks and a trace consisting of 10 ft of 175-lb. cable-laid wire and a small hook. Having lost many good sharks through poor wire he concludes that the porbeagle that come inshore are very timid and can be put off easily by a hook which is so mounted as to be obvious. He has found that when there are mackerel about, the bait must be kept moving or the shark will completely ignore it, which strengthens the idea that the porbeagle is a sight-feeder.

As the reader will have realized, there is a high degree of patience and perseverance required for this fishing. The sharks sometimes desert inshore waters for long periods and many sharkless days are inevitable. But one 100-lb. shark from the shore would surely be worth all the frustrations and disappointments.

9. CAUTION

Whether fishing from a boat or from the shore, whether the shark is still in the water or out of it, alive or apparently dead, it is advisable to treat any type of shark, big or small, with the utmost respect. If an angler becomes careless even for a moment when handling his shark he is most certainly asking for trouble. Even a very small shark's mouth is a deadly weapon. So when the shark has been gaffed and boated, anglers should stay well clear of the head as it comes inboard, because it can whip around with surprising speed and if the teeth only so much as graze any part of a man's body the consequences can be ugly. I was once a witness to this. A small blue shark of about 30 lb., gaffed in the stomach, had been turned on the gaff for a photograph. The man holding the gaff turned the shark's head towards himself instead of away and as it passed his thigh, the mouth simply opened and closed. Luckily only the top teeth came in contact with the man's flesh for just a split second as it was being turned, but he received a razor-like cut about six inches long and so deep it reached the thigh bone.

Even when the shark has been knocked on the head and is lying motionless in the boat it can involuntarily open and close its mouth without any warning. It is therefore dangerous for an angler who at this point is trying to remove a hook and he could suffer a very severe injury. This happened to a friend of mine when he tried to remove a hook from a porbeagle that had been dead for over fifteen minutes — but for fast medical attention his hand would have been lost. The teeth of the blue shark, designed as cutting instruments, are so dangerous that even to rub one's finger along one is sufficient to cause a gash.

The tail must also be closely watched for a

A very dangerous situation is captured by the camera. As the boatman was lifting in Clive Gammon's shark, a large wave struck the boat and caused him to lose balance.

slap from a thresher, mako or porbeagle can break a leg if caught at an awkward angle.

The most important thing to remember when handling shark is to respect them for the terribly efficient killing machines which nature has designed them to be.

10. RESEARCH AND CONSERVATION

Through the ages man has learned that too much exploitation will doom any natural resource. In order to establish just how much depletion a resource can take it is necessary to find out, firstly how abundant it is, secondly if some of it were removed how soon could it be replaced naturally, and thirdly would its removal have any harmful side-effects on any other resource? For the past hundred years or so scientists have been doing this type of research on the fishes of our seas, and even though they tell us that many species are doomed to extinction if exploitation continues at the present rate, the governments of the world are doing nothing seriously to check the threat. Unfortunately for sea anglers little work has been done on the life history of the various non-commercial species such as shark, skate, bream, tope, monkfish and many others which are now becoming of major importance for a new reason — sport. With this lack of knowledge in mind the Irish Government, through the Inland Fisheries Trust, has embarked on a research programme to establish the life history of the various sea fish which are important to anglers, and primary among these fish are the blue and the porbeagle shark.

As well as trying to establish the growth rate, age at maturity and food of these two species, it is also necessary to know their migratory habits. In 1970 a tagging programme was started and continues on the south and west coasts of Ireland. As I was doing most of the tagging some of the things I have learned would be of interest to shark anglers. In the 1972 Annual Report of the Inland Fisheries Trust, we showed that there was a very close connection between sea-water temperature and the number of blue shark present. Both the water temperature at surface level and the number of shark tagged were recorded daily. When logged at the end of the season these figures showed that when the water was between 13° C. and 13·5° C. an average of 1·3 blues were tagged each day; between 14° C. and 14·5° C. there were 7; between 15° C. and 15·5° C., 21·3; and between 16° C. and 16·5° C., 21·8. This suggests that even in the middle of summer it is not worth while fishing for blues if the temperature is much below 14° C. and the warmer it gets the better the catch. The temperature must be taken on the open sea and not in the harbour or enclosed area.

The second observation is that blue shark remain in the rubby-dubby trail for many hours swimming up and down looking for food. It is therefore likely that if a shark is seen in the trail but vanishes without taking the bait he will return within a few hours and take it. This was established in 1972 when a new system of tagging was devised. Prior to 1972 all sharks were hooked, played to the side of the boat, tagged through the dorsal fin and released whether the hook had been removed or left inside. There were some doubts about the survival chances of shark tagged in such a manner because of possible internal damage caused by the necessary rough handling at the side of the boat or because of the shark's violent regurgitating in his effort to throw the hook. It has been suggested that when fighting, a shark can accumulate so much lactic acid in his bloodstream that it can ultimately poison him. In order to overcome these problems a system of 'free tagging' was devised, which entailed attracting the shark right up to the boat by using good rubby dubby and harpooning it beside the dorsal